I'M

FOR

LIFE...

WITHOUT

APOLOGY.

JOHNNY A PALMER JR

Thesis: Abortion has becoming an acceptable practice in our present day culture. This practice has been presented in a deceptive, watered down fashion. Many have been brain washed into thinking that Abortion is something less than what it is, murder. This is incompatible with Biological and Biblical truth, and therefore, if pursued it will have grave consequences.

I. The Background *Concerning* Abortion.

A. *Definitions*.

B. *Descriptions*.

C. Legal *Decisions*.

II. The Biological *Considerations* of Abortion.

A. *Examining* the *Child* from conception onward.

B. *Excuses Commonly* used.

III. The Biblical *Condemnation* of Abortion.

A. God's *Viewpoint* of when life begins.

B. God's *Value* placed on life.

C. God's *Vengeance* for Taking life.

IV. Beyond the present *Concerns* of Abortion.

A. Future Permissiveness.

B. Future Judgment

C. Future possibility of Revival.

To start our research concerning abortion, we must begin by defining some relevant terms. First, let us look at the word "life." There are, without a doubt, many different viewpoints as to the meaning, value, and beginning of life. Once I was told by a man "life begins at forty", clever; however, those at forty would readily admit that is somewhat crude. Later, we will examine it biologically as well as biblically. Indeed, many of us have strange ideas concerning the value of life. Nobody seems to want to live to be a hundred-except those, of course, who are ninety-nine. Anyway, let us look at a few definitions concerning life. Webster defines life as "living things", simple but unfortunately not overly helpful. A scientist would use different terms like this: "Being alive depends on sharing this list of material characteristics. Anything that lacks an important part of this basic list is, by that token, not fully alive." [1] Another definition is that "Life is something that is happening. It is a process." [2] It becomes evident that life can be hard to define in a simple easy way. Yet we shall clearly see without any doubt that a child in the mother's womb is definitely alive from conception onward. We will also find that this life is very precious to God.

Secondly, we must then define abortion. This, too, is defined in many ways by many different people. However, this is a much easier term to nail down. Dr. Charles C. Ryrie defines abortion as "the expulsion of the human fetus prematurely (that is, before it is capable of surviving outside the womb)." [3] It should be understood that we are not dealing with unplanned abortion but rather planned or induced abortion - willful.

I personally feel comfortable with defining planned abortion as pure and simple murder. It is taking that which is alive and willfully putting him/her to death.

Thirdly, by way of background let us consider abortion in light of its legality. In many civilizations gone by, abortion has been an accepted practice. "In the pagan Roman Empire abortion was freely practiced, but Christians took a stand against it. [4] It would be very refreshing if we would seek to learn from the mistakes of the past instead of foolishly falling into their errors. For the sake of importance and space, we will deal with our present culture and civilization. It is most appalling to observe our legal system, which has slowly become degenerate and deceived. For example in 1959, the United Nations passed a resolution, which states, "The child, by reason of its physical and mental immaturity, needs special safeguards and care, including appropriate legal protection before as well as after birth." [5] The Supreme Court, in days or years gone by, upheld such things as public prayer, human rights even when one, such as an unborn cannot speak. Yet in 1963, the Court ruled out all prayer in public schools. To even mention one's favor for capital punishment is an embarrassment thanks to the Supreme Court's decision that it is extraordinary and cruel punishment. I am afraid our Supreme Court has often done more damage than good, as is seen in a Brooklyn case:

In Brooklyn, N.Y., the wife and five small children of Jose Suarez 23 years old, were found butchered in their Brooklyn apartment. Suarez was arrested, but he denied even knowing the mother and her children. He was discharged but rearrested on the same day. That night he confessed to the six murders. An assistant district attorney was present when he confessed, but the confessed murderer was not told before he was questioned of his right to have an attorney present. Suarez appeared before State Supreme Court Justice Michael Kern. According to the ruling of Earl Warren's Supreme Court, there was nothing that the judge could do but turn the murderer loose—to go his own free way and to do whatever his depraved mind prompted him to do." [6]

It seems the Court is worried about everyone's rights except for the defenseless and innocent. Perhaps the most discouraging decision yet is the judgment concerning abortion when "the Supreme Court decided in January 1973 that the unborn child had absolutely no rights." [7] They are always debating whether our tax dollars will pay for abortion on demand.

Righteousness exalts a nation, but sin is a disgrace to *any* people. Proverbs 14:34

I believe we are now opening the very door to the judgment of Almighty God. We are no Longer one Nation under God, but we have become a god unto ourselves!   As Dr. Graham has stated, "If God doesn't judge America; He'll have to apologize to Sodom and Gomorrah." The main point is that although abortion is presently legal that hardly makes it right.

Next, it is absolutely essential that we determine the state of the child within the womb from a biological perspective. "Despite the Supreme Court ruling, it is recognized medically and biologically that human life is present at the moment of implantation [conception] (when the fertilized ovum embeds itself in the wall of the uterus)... [8] In order to develop this fact it will be valuable to trace development of the child from conception on. The best way to do this is to present "significant events in a new life":

Chronology of the Human Mother [9]

- Date of last menstrual period

1. Immediately upon fertilization cellular development begins.

2. At Implantation, the new life is composed of hundreds of cells.

- 2 Weeks, ovulation--conception-fertilization

3. At 17 days, the new life has

developed its own blood cells..."

4. 19 days, eyes start to develop.

- 5-9 days, implantation in the uterus of mother.

5. 20 days, the foundation of the entire nervous system has been laid down.

6. 24 days, heart has regular beats.

- 14 days (approx.) the first menstrual period is missed.

7. 28 days, 40 pairs of muscles are developed along the trunk of the new life; arm and legs are forming.

8. 30 days, regular blood flow within the vascular system; the ears & nasal development have begun.

9. 40 days, the heart energy output is reported to be almost 20% of an adult.
10. 42 days skeleton complete and reflexes are present.

11. 43 days, electrical brain wave patterns can be recorded. This is usually ample evidence that thinking is taking place in the brain.

12. 49 days, the appearance of a miniature doll with complete fingers, toes, and ears.

- 28 days after conception earliest test for pregnancy.

13. Name Changed from Embryo To Fetus. At 56 days all organs functioning and intact.

- Six weeks after conception, testing for pregnancy relatively reliable. Mother has physical signs of pregnancy and is wondering if she is going to have second missed period or is truly pregnant.

14. 9th & 10th week, squints, swallows, retracts tongue.

15. 11th & 12th week, arms and legs move, sucks thumb, inhales and exhales

amniotic fluid..."

16. 16 weeks genital organs clearly differentiated, grasps with hands, swims, kicks and turns somersaults.

- Eight weeks after conception, reported by some anti-life proponents as only a glob of tissue.

17. 18 weeks, vocal cords working, can cry.

18. 20 weeks, hair appears on head; weight—one pound; height-12 in.

These biological facts speak for themselves, life begins at conception and grows at a rather fast pace onward.

The first stage of the child is commonly called the Embryo stage. It is this period which generally ranges from conception until about the 8th week. Many things happen during this period as has been observed. It is very important to notice that the child is genetically complete, and his or her physical features are already determined. The second stage of the child is referred to as a Fetus stage. By this time, we see that all vital organs are functioning and intact. The remaining time is for preparation, for the child to be brought forth into the world. It is interesting to denote that the child can survive outside the womb as early as six months. It should, with these undeniable truths be obviously clear that we are talking about not only potential life but also presently alive babies from conception on.

Abortion is therefore the taking, of a defenseless life. These murders are done in various ways. One common method is called curettage. "In this technique, which is carried out between the seventh and twelfth weeks of pregnancy, the uterus is approached through the vagina...the surgeon then scrapes the wall of the uterus, cutting the baby's body to pieces and scraping the placenta from its attachments..." [10] Another way of execution is called salt poisoning, "This method is done after 16 weeks when enough fluid has accumulated in the sac around the baby. A long, needle is inserted through the mother's abdomen into the baby's sac and a solution of concentrated salt is injected into it. The baby breathes in and swallows the salt and is poisoned by it..." [11] A third way and perhaps most crude is referred to as the Hysterotomy way. Dr. Koop noted, "A hysterotomy is exactly the same as a cesarean section with the one difference, namely, that in a cesarean section the operation is being done to save, the life of the baby whereas in the hysterotomy the operation is being done to kill the baby." [12] The methods themselves are not the issue, whether one is poisoned or cut to pieces the verdict is still, murder plain and simple. It is frightful to realize that the primary cause of death in the United States has often been abortion." [3]

These biological facts help to clear up some common, misunderstandings which, abortionists have, namely the familiar cry—"It's my body, and I have the right to do with it what I want to." However, this is not biologically true. We must come to grips with the plain vanilla facts, the baby is Not part of the mother's body. Koop says, "The child in the womb is not a part of the woman's

body, subject to her absolute control. She provides the environment and the sustenance but this sustenance does not go to a subhuman creature devoid of human rights. [14] It must also be noted, that one-half of the child belongs to the Father. This is a fact that seems to be overlooked by those who sing this song. In conclusion, we must not forget the most important fact of all, the child is a person. It seems strange that the Supreme Court would refer to the yet unborn child as a "non-person" on one hand, yet at the same time the mother of that same child or "non-person" can bring a paternity suit into action. This same so-called "non-person" can, if injured in an accident, sue the one who brought the harm after the actual birth, when this "non-person" as the Court mistakenly calls him or her suddenly becomes a person! It becomes very apparent that our legal system is full of contradictions and lacks common sense. Perhaps it should be required for all court officials to, take an elementary course in biology.
Now, let us consider the Biblical aspects of abortion. This is the most important

subject to be discussed. The Bible is the ultimate and final authority. The only way to measure, whether something is right or wrong, good or bad is by the Word of God. There will be some, of course who do not believe the validity of the Word of God. This really avoids the issue, God's word is true whether man believes it or not!

3 What then? If some did not believe, their unbelief will not nullify the faithfulness of God, will it? 4 May it never be! Rather, let God be found true, though every man *be found* a liar... 15

Everyone will give an account to God regardless of one's personal opinion. We will not judge the Bible, it will in fact, judge us. So with that in mind, let us examine abortion in the light of scripture.

First of all there are some who would have us believe that the Bible is almost silent on this issue, this is not true if one keeps the proper understanding of what we are really dealing with, that being out and out murder. And "the Bible screams from cover to cover that life is precious to God. Texts such as Psalm 139:12-16; Isaiah 44:1-2, 24; Jeremiah 1:5 and Exodus 4:10 should be preached from our evangelical pulpits" [16] says Dr. Koop. This is indeed an accurate statement, as we shall now observe.

Secondly, we must come to see that life, which is precious to God, according to God, begins long before physical birth:

[12] Even the darkness is not dark to You, And the night is as bright as the day. Darkness and light are alike *to You.* [13] For You formed my inward parts; You wove me in my mother's womb. [14] I will give thanks to You, for I am fearfully and wonderfully made; Wonderful are Your works, And my soul knows it very well. [15] My frame was not hidden from You, When I was made in secret, *And* skillfully wrought in the depths of the earth; Psalm 139:12-15

See also Gen. 9:6 and Mat. 1:18-20.

This verse reveals the fact that God is concerned for life in the womb. It reveals His protection and possession concerning the unborn.

[1] "But now listen, O Jacob, My servant, And Israel, whom I have chosen: [2] Thus says the LORD who made you And formed you from the womb, who will help you, 'Do not fear, O Jacob My servant; And you Jeshurun whom I have chosen. Isaiah 44:1-2

[4] Now the word of the LORD came to me saying, [5] "Before I formed you in the womb I knew you, And before you were born I consecrated you; I have appointed you a prophet to the nations." Jeremiah 1:4-5

This clearly shows God's plan and purpose for man prior to actual birth. From this passage, it is very clear that God would not have been pleased had someone tried to perform an abortion, on Mrs. Jeremiah.

[5] Behold, I was brought forth in iniquity, And in sin my mother conceived me. Psalm 51:5

"David confesses that he was conceived in sin. The iniquity and sin meant are not those of his mother, but his own. This important passage establishes the humanness of the fetus since guilt is attached to it." [17]

[23] The LORD said to her, "Two nations are in your womb; And two peoples will be separated from your body; And one people shall be stronger than the other; And the older shall serve the younger." Genesis 25:23

[41] When Elizabeth heard Mary's greeting, the baby leaped in her womb; and Elizabeth was filled with the Holy Spirit. Luke 1:41

These scriptures speak for themselves and really need little interpretation. Life without a doubt in God's eyes begins in the womb. Another important verse is found in Exodus 21:22-24. Here we see that life in the womb is to be protected and valued.

[22] "If men struggle with each other and strike a woman with child so that she gives birth prematurely, yet there is no

injury, he shall surely be fined as the woman's husband may demand of him, and he shall pay as the judges *decide.* [23] "But if there is *any further* injury, then you shall appoint *as a penalty* life for life. Exodus 21:22-23

This again shows that the fetus is definitely regarded in scripture as a person. Meredith G. Kline in an article stated "Exod 21:22-25 turns out to be perhaps the most decisive positive evidence in Scripture that the fetus is to be regarded as a living person." [18]
There are some that point out the fact that the punishment for causing the death of the fetus was merely a fine and not death. This at first would seem to be a valid point but this cannot really be compared to abortion as was pointed out by Barbara Deane:

That's really stretching a point. I don't think this is abortion. It's accidental—what might be called manslaughter. However, I think abortion is premeditated, such as a first degree murder in which you definitely set out to perform a lethal act...you don't accidentally destroy the life of a fetus when you perform an abortion. You purposefully do it. [19]

Finally, we must look at God's view of man's willfully ending life. This of course is called plain and simply murder. We should therefore briefly look at several passages concerning this subject:

Thou shall not kill. Exodus 20:13 This would better be translated. Thou shall not murder. To kill does carry with it the idea of justification. For example, if you shoot a squirrel, for food, during squirrel season, it could be said that you killed a squirrel. This is also true of those in the armed forces who might have to kill, for the safety and survival of our country. Murder on the other hand does not have any justification.

[16] There are six things which the LORD hates, Yes, seven which are an abomination to Him: [17] Haughty eyes, a lying tongue, And hands that shed innocent blood, Proverbs 6:16-17

¹⁵ Make sure that none of you suffers as a murderer, or thief, or evildoer, or a troublesome meddler; 1 Peter 4:15

⁷ "He who overcomes will inherit these things, and I will be his God and he will be My son. ⁸ "But for the cowardly and unbelieving and abominable and murderers and immoral persons and sorcerers and idolaters and all liars, their part *will be* in the lake that burns with fire and brimstone, which is the second death." Revelation 21:7-8

It must be kept in mind that people will spend eternity in hell, separated from God, not because of abortion, adultery or the like. People are eternally lost because of their rejection of the Lord Jesus Christ. Nevertheless, these few passages clearly show that Murderers can definitely expect God's judgment if they enter eternity without applying the blood of the Lord Jesus Christ. If you have had an abortion you can come to Christ and find pardon and imputed righteousness. After all much of the Bible was written by murderers – Moses, David, and Paul. This is not to make light of murder, but to focus on God's gracious gift of salvation through the Person and Work of the Lord Jesus Christ. If you have had an abortion, I hope you will read the last chapter of this book and find love, acceptance, and forgiveness through Christ. However, if you reject God's love and forgiveness offered you, you will experience God's wrath in time and eternity. I pray that will not be your eternal destination.

Lastly, we must consider what lies beyond the abortion issue, and, as Christians, our response and responsibility to take a stand. Where does all of this lead? Is there Justifiable concern that the abortion issue is the door to future degeneration? The answer is, without a doubt, yes!

First, it can lead to the value of life itself, as we know it, to be terminated. People become less personal and more disposable as their usefulness wears out. Dr. Koop notes, "It takes almost nothing to move from abortion, which is the killing of an unborn baby in the uterus, to the killing of the retarded, the crippled, the sick, the elderly." [20] Could we actually put to death human beings made in God's Image because they are no longer an asset? This is a frightful thought indeed but not far from a reality. This free-will murder that has the handicapped and elderly as their main target assumes that because someone is unwanted or unneeded it is ok to kill, or a better term would be to murder them. With this sick attitude, we would eliminate half the population in a matter of days. If this sounds far out, consider this, to a certain extent such children who are deformed are being, murdered right here and now in the United States of America.

We must remember that God is sovereign, and he decides the affairs of man:

[11] The LORD said to him, "Who has made man's mouth? Or who makes *him* mute or deaf, or seeing or blind? Is it not I, the LORD? [12] "Now then go, and I, even I, will be with your mouth, and teach you what you are to say."
Exodus 4:11-12

God decides the outcome of our lives according to His unsearchable wisdom God has the right to do anything and everything He pleases, but it can be also said anything and everything He does is always right!

^{34} "But at the end of that period, I, Nebuchadnezzar, raised my eyes toward heaven and my reason returned to me, and I blessed the Most High and praised and honored Him who lives forever; For His dominion is an everlasting dominion, And His kingdom *endures* from generation to generation. ^{35} "All the inhabitants of the earth are accounted as nothing, But He does according to His will in the host of heaven And *among* the inhabitants of earth; And no one can ward off His hand Or say to Him, 'What have You done?' Daniel 4:34-35

^{3} But our God is in the heavens; He does whatever He pleases. Psalm 115:3

We must always believe that God knows best. It should be encouraging to us that God's strength is perfected in our weakness! And if one is deformed from birth it is by God's design and plan. It must also avoid a false conclusion concerning the happiness of those who are physically or mentally troubled. Think of people such as Franklin Roosevelt, Napoleon, Helen Keller, or perhaps someone in your own family who was thought at one time not to have a meaningful life, yet, with the passage of time made fantastic contributions to history.

We also cannot conclude that because one is born with a handicap that they will remain that way.

"The blind man of John 9 was born that way, and although the disciples, following a common belief of the times, thought that this was a punishment for sin the Lord clearly stated that it was so the works of God should be made manifest in him (Jn. 9:3). Now try to think of the implications of the following line of reasoning...Suppose a prenatal test could have shown that this baby boy was to be born without sight. The parents might have been advised to consider sparing themselves the problems of rearing such a child by terminating the pregnancy, supposing abortion was easily and legally available in Palestine. Should they abort the fetus or not? Imagine, further, that they did decide to have the abortion. Obviously the baby would not have been born, the child would not have grown up and he would not have been the means of demonstrating the works of God. [21]

This is not an isolated case found in the gospels; surely, Jesus healed many who were born, with deformities and handicaps.

[2] And a man who had been lame from his mother's womb was being carried along, whom they used to set down every day at the gate of the temple which is called Beautiful, in order to beg alms of those who were entering the temple. [3] When he saw Peter and John about to go into the temple, he *began* asking to receive alms. [4] But Peter, along with John, fixed his gaze on him and said, "Look at us!" [5] And he *began* to give them his attention, expecting to receive something from them. [6] But Peter said, "I do not possess silver and

gold, but what I do have I give to you: In the name of Jesus Christ the Nazarene—walk!" 7 And seizing him by the right hand, he raised him up; and immediately his feet and his ankles were strengthened. 8 With a leap he stood upright and *began* to walk; and he entered the temple with them, walking and leaping and praising God. Acts 3:2-8

Next, abortion can be harmful to the mother involved in several different ways. First of all it can be harmful physically "there has been a rising incidence of premature births due to cervical scarring, which is one of the results of repeated abortions." [22] Secondly, it can affect them mentally because many have tremendous guilt afterward. Guilt is always a very destructive force and impossible to live with, without repercussions. One young woman who had gotten an abortion said, "I felt relieved not to be pregnant and was ready to start life again. But My Trouble was just beginning. At home I was inconsiderate and belligerent. I was mean even to Rich. My schoolwork

==slipped, and I couldn't cope with my position as editor of the school paper. Though I blocked memories of the abortion, I know now that this probably caused my depression and self-hatred.==
23

The cost of an abortion is tremendous!

In conclusion, it is time for Christians to take a stand. We cannot be passive any longer. First, we have the privilege of prayer. The situation on the surface seems almost irrevocable, however, we must realize that God is still on His Throne and has promised to honor the fervent prayers of His people:

[3] 'Call to Me and I will answer you, and I will tell you great and mighty things, which you do not know.' Jeremiah 33:3

[17] 'Ah Lord GOD! Behold, You have made the heavens and the earth by Your great power and by Your outstretched arm! Nothing is too difficult for You, Jeremiah 32:17

Has God not already begun to answer our prayers by giving us Mike Pence as vice president? A Christian who is clearly Pro-Life.

We must pray for National Repentance, I believe Revival among God's people and evangelism to the lost is our only hope. Of course there is the Blessed Hope of God taking the church out of here in the Rapture (1 Thess. 4:16-18).

Secondly, we can be informed so that we can calmly and confidently share the biblical view to those who are confused; we should use every means possible – radio; television; the pulpit; books; etc.

Thirdly, we can work through our governmental system, by petitions, letters to proper authorities, and even seeking an amendment.

We are at the crossroads. It is time to Repent or Perish, this Nation by God's grace could truly be one nation under God.

The greatness of America lies not in being more enlightened than any other nation, but rather in her ability to repair her faults. —Alexis de Tocqueville

A Child's Hope, by Jean Wauby

I did not ask to be wanted
And I know I am not
I did not ask to be born,
And I know I will never be
I did not ask to live,
And I know that before I live,
I will die.

You are the only world I know
But you do not want me.
You know they will kill me
But you do not stop them.
I do not understand.
I want to live, to be free,
And you have no right
To take that right from me.

When they kill me, look at me,
And you who kill me look at me,
Look carefully.
See, I have tiny fingers,
I have feet, hands, and a heart that was
beating a moment ago.

My body is intricate as yours,
But because I am helpless I have no say
Not even to cry, "Don't make me die!"

But I have one hope;
The right to take life you stole.
That right belongs to God alone;
And I know that God is just,
And I know that He is merciful.

Because of this I can hope.
This is hope for me,
But you who kill me,
You too will die,
And then will your hope
Be as great as mine?

Footnotes

1. Stanley L. Weinberg, <u>Biology: An Inquiry into the Nature of Life</u> (Ally and Bacon Inc., 1974), p.5

2. Grolier, <u>The Book of Knowledge</u> (New York: Grolier Inc., 1971), p. 209

3. Charles C. Ryrie, <u>You Mean the Bible Teaches That...</u> (Chicago, Illinois: by Moody Press, 1974), p. 85

4. Francis A. Schaeffer, How Shall We Then Live? (Old Tappan, New Jersey: Fleming H. Revell Company, 1976), p. 36

5. Everett C. Koop, The Right to Live; the Right to Die (Wheaton, Illinois: Tyndale House Publishers, Inc., 1976), p. 36

6. Paul Lee Tan, Signs of the Times (Rockville, Maryland: Assurance Publisher, 1979), #3745

7. Koop, p. 14

8. Harold O.J. Brown, The American Way of Death (Moody Monthly Magazine, 1976), p. 32

9. Pro-Life Material, Significant Events in a New Life.
10. Koop, p. 30

11. Pro-Life Material, Life or Death

12. Koop, p. 31

13. Moody Monthly, p. 32

14. Koop, p. 59

15. Romans 3:3-4 NAS

16. Everett C. Koop, <u>Abortion</u> (United Evangelical Action), p. 15

17. Ryrie, p. 89

18. Meredith G. Kline, <u>Lex Talionis and the Human Fetus</u> (Journal of the Evangelical Theological Society, 1977), p. 193

19. Barbara Dean, <u>Murder</u> (Logos Journal), p. 47

20. Koop, p. 79

21. Ryrie, p. 90

22. Koop, p. 47

23. Anonymous, <u>For Me, Abortion Was Wrong</u> (Moody Monthly, 1976), p. 37

24. Paul Lee Tan, #7018

Gospel Presentation:

Let me ask you one of the most important questions you will ever ponder.

Have you come to a place in your life where you know for certain that if you died you would go to heaven?

The only answer to that question is, yes, no, or I don't know. Take a moment and think about it. A follow up question would be:'

If you were standing before God right now and He were to ask, "Why should I let you into my perfect heaven?"

What do you think you would say? You might say, "I go to church. I try to live a good life. I try to keep God's law." Such responses are sincere, and I appreciate your honesty. Most would probably say, "I don't know what I would say." Well, would you like to know? Then read the following carefully.

God Really Does Love You

"For God so loved the world, (put your name here), that He gave His only begotten Son, that whoever believes in Him should not perish but have everlasting life" (John 3:16).

It is natural to question this claim; we tend to wonder how God could love us with all of our problems and hang-ups, yes, you can say it – with all of our sins. My wife and I have had two children. When they were born they did nothing for us! And after they were born, for the first several months they kept us up all hours of the night; we had to change their diapers and feed them. I think most of you know what I'm talking about. However, we did love them. Why? I suppose it was because we had something to do with them being in this world. They are our children; they even looked a little like us – poor kids! You need to realize that God is the one who had everything to do with your coming into this world. Without God you would not even exist! He is the Creator and Sustainer of life. He, in fact, created you in His image and loves you even though you have done nothing to deserve it.

So What's a Fella to Do?

Have you ever felt that your life lacked purpose and meaning? Have these thoughts ever crossed your mind:

- Where did I come from?
- Why am I here?
- Where am I going?

God knows the answer to these questions. He created you with a definite purpose in mind.

"The thief does not come except to steal, and to kill, and to destroy. I have come that they may have life, and that they may have it more abundantly" (John 10:10).

An abundant life is a life of purpose, meaning, and fulfillment. That is what God offers you. This brings up an unavoidable question—what happened! If He loves us and has this great purpose for our life, then why are both concepts so foreign to us? The answer is both profound and very simple.

Sin Separates!

We are all sinners, "for all have sinned and fall short of the glory of God" (Rom. 3:22). We are a sinner by birth. God created Adam and Eve and put them in a garden with only one commandment; they were not to eat of a certain tree. They disobeyed God by taking a bite, and thus they sinned. Now what kind of babies are two sinful people capable of having? It is the law of biogenesis—like produces like. This is why there is no need to teach children how to tell a lie, but only to teach them positive things like telling the truth. They know how to lie naturally!
The reason for that is that we are all born with a sin nature inherited from Adam.

"Therefore, just as through one man sin entered the world, and death through sin, and thus death spread to all men, because all sinned" (Rom. 5:12).

We are also sinners by behavior. Have you not sinned? The Bible commands us to love God with all our heart, mind, and soul. Have you always done that? Have you ever done that? Have you ever told a lie? Have you ever wanted to? God not only looks at our deeds but at our desires. The Bible clearly declares we have all sinned.

So What?

Here is the answer to the so-what question.

"For the wages of sin is death, but the gift of God is eternal life in Christ Jesus our Lord" (Rom. 6:23).

What we have earned from our sin is death. Death means separation.

- There is spiritual death—the separation of the spirit/soul from God. "And the LORD God commanded the man, saying, 'Of every tree of the garden you may freely eat; but of the tree of the knowledge of good and evil you shall not eat, for in the day that you eat of it you shall surely die'" (Gen. 2:16–17). The day they ate of it they did not physically die; that took place many years later. But God said *in the day* you eat of it you will die. They died spiritually that very day.

- There is also physical death—the separation of the spirit/soul from the body. "And as it is appointed for men to die once, but after this the judgment" (Heb. 9:27). The fact that everybody dies physically is proof positive that everyone is spiritually dead. If we were not sinners, we would not die. The statistics are rather impressive; one out of every one person dies!

- If you die physically while you are spiritually dead, you will die eternally. Eternal death is the eternal separation of the spirit/soul/body from God's goodness, grace, mercy, and blessings. It is to be fully conscious and live in a place the Bible calls the lake of fire. "Then Death and Hades were cast into the lake of fire. This is the second death. And anyone not found written in the Book of Life was cast into the lake of fire" (Rev. 20:14–15).

Question: How can you say one moment that God loves me and then in the next that He condemns me?

Well let us imagine putting on a judge's robe and sitting on the bench. Then the unthinkable happens. Your son, whom you love very much, is brought before you, guilty of a capital offense! The penalty for his crime is death, and the evidence is clear as to his guilt. Would you sentence him to death? If you were a just judge, you would, not because you no longer love him, but in spite of your great love for him. God is holy, righteous, and just, as well as a God of love. This looks like bad news! However, the very word *gospel* means good news, so where is this good news?

Jesus Christ Is God

"In the beginning was the Word, and the Word was with God, and the Word was God" (John 1:1).

This is a great mystery, but the Bible teaches that God became God/man. "And the Word became flesh and dwelt among us, and we beheld His glory, the glory as of the only begotten of the Father, full of grace and truth" (John 1:14).

Jesus Christ the Substitute

The Lord Jesus Christ lived a perfect life and then died in your place. "But God demonstrates His own love toward us, in that while we were still sinners, Christ died for us" (Rom. 5:8 NKJV).

Let us put our judge robe back on for a minute. Imagine after sentencing your boy to be executed, taking off your robe and then voluntarily offering to die in his place. That would make you just and loving at the same time. That is what Jesus Christ actually did for us. We do not understand all of this but must accept it by faith. I do not understand electricity, but I still do not live in the dark. I do not understand how the digestive system works, but I still eat. I do not understand how a brown cow eats green grass and produces white milk. You do not have to understand everything to be saved—just that you are a sinner and that Jesus Christ died for your sin.

He Is Not Here, He Has Risen

"For I delivered to you first of all that which I also received: that Christ died for our sins according to the Scriptures, and that He was buried, and that He rose again the third day according to the Scriptures, and that He was seen by Cephas, then by the twelve. After that He was seen by over five hundred brethren at once, of whom the greater part remain to the present, but some have fallen asleep" (1 Cor. 15:3–6).

By rising from the dead, He proved that He paid for all of our sins. If He had not, death would have held Him. It also proved that He had no sin of His own. If

He had, He would have stayed dead like everybody else.

One Way Only

We have all seen *One Way Only* signs, and so it is with the way of salvation. There is only one person who can save. "Jesus said to him, 'I am the way, the truth, and the life. No one comes to the Father except through Me'" (John 14:6).

You can line up every one of us on the West Coast with plans to swim to Hawaii, and no doubt, some would swim a lot farther than others. Nevertheless, we would all have one thing in common: nobody would make it! It is impossible for anybody to swim from the West Coast to Hawaii. And it is just as impossible for sinful man to make his way to a Holy God on his own without experiencing God's wrath. What one needs is a boat to get them from the West Coast to Hawaii. Moreover, the only salvation boat is the Lord Jesus Christ. That Jesus is the only way to be saved is as true as $2 + 2 = 4$. There is only one answer to that equation, and there is only one way to be saved.

"Nor is there salvation in any other, for there is no other name under heaven given among men by which we must be saved" (Acts 4:12).

Facts

These are only facts. Giving mental assent to these facts is not enough to save anyone. It is not enough to give intellectual assent to these facts. We must believe and thus receive Christ.

"But as many as received Him, to them He gave the right to become children of God, to those who believe in His name" (John 1:12).

Faith

Facts must be wedded to faith. So, what do we mean when we say believe or place your faith in Christ?

Faith involves mind, emotion, and will.

Years ago, a tightrope walker named Charles Blondin, went across Niagara Falls, walking on a wire. He went back and forth. He even filled a wheelbarrow with bricks and took that across. A crowd gathered, and he asked one of them, "Do you believe I could do that with you?" The man agreed that he could. Then Blondin said, "Hop on in, and I'll carry you across." The man said, "No way!" You see, he did not really believe. He believed in his mind that Blondin could take him across; he wanted him to in his emotions, but he would not commit himself to Blondin and trust him to take him across. Saving faith involves our mind, emotion, and will.

Amazing Grace

You likely have heard the song, "Amazing Grace." We are saved by grace through faith in Jesus Christ. Now faith is not a work—faith is to believe in the work of another. "For by grace you have been saved through faith, and that not of yourselves; it is the gift of

God, not of works, lest anyone should boast" (Eph. 2:8–9).

Dr. Gerstner: "Christ has done everything necessary for his salvation. Nothing now stands between the sinner and God but the sinner's good works. Nothing can keep him from Christ but his delusion that he does not need Him—that he has good works of his own that can satisfy God. If men will only be convinced that all their righteousness is as filthy rags; if men will see that there is none that does good, no, not one; if men will see that all are shut up under sin—then there will be nothing to prevent their everlasting salvation. All they need is need. All they must have is nothing. All that is required is acknowledged guilt. But alas, sinners cannot part from their virtues. They are imaginary, but they are real to them. So grace becomes unreal. The real grace of God they spurn in order to hold on to the illusory virtues of their own. Their eyes fixed on a mirage; they will not drink real water. They die of thirst in the midst of an ocean of grace."

Repentance is a synonym for faith; it is like heads and tails of *one* coin. Repentance is not making a vow you will stop sinning, nor is it a change of life. You cannot stop sinning or change your life until God saves you! I have fished most of my life and I have never cleaned a fish before I caught it. Repentance is a *change of mind*, about who you are, a sinner; and about the Lord Jesus Christ, the only one who can save you based on His death, burial, and resurrection.

Good Enough Is Not Good Enough

The religious leaders of Jesus' day prayed three times a week, fasted twice a week, never missed going to the house of worship, and memorized the Old Testament (Luke 18:9–12). Yet, Jesus said that if you are not more righteous then they, you are not going to make it!

"For I say to you, that unless your righteousness exceeds the righteousness of the scribes and

Pharisees, you will by no means enter the kingdom of heaven (Matt. 5:20).

Then he says something rather startling:

"Therefore you shall be perfect, just as your Father in heaven is perfect" (Matt. 5:48).

Did you know Jesus said it takes perfect righteousness to get to heaven? We all know that nobody is perfect! How then can we be perfectly righteous before a perfectly righteous God?

"For He made Him who knew no sin to be sin for us, that we might become the righteousness of God in Him" (2 Cor. 5:21).

The truth is, there is only one person who lived a perfect life, and that was Jesus Christ. You see, the good news is that not only did Jesus die on the cross in our place, to offer us forgiveness of all our sins, He also offers us His perfect righteousness, placed on our account! The only sin Jesus ever knew was ours;

the only righteousness we will ever know is His.

Never the Same!

Salvation is not an external thing. When you receive Jesus Christ as your Savior, He makes you a new creature within!

"Therefore, if anyone is in Christ, he is a new creation; old things have passed away; behold, all things have become new" (2 Cor. 5:17).
And the Holy Spirit takes up permanent residence within you.

"And because you are sons, God has sent forth the Spirit of His Son into your hearts, crying out, 'Abba, Father'" (Gal. 4:6).

Thus, you now have the desire (new nature) and the power (indwelling Holy Spirit) to live for God. You are positionally changed from being in Adam to now being in Christ, and experientially changed because the inner transformation of regeneration and salvation begins the process of progressive sanctification, which ultimately leads to glorification.

"For it is God who works in you both to will and to do for His good pleasure" (Phil. 2:13).

While we still have an old sin nature though Satan is opposing us every step of the way, we must grow in the grace and knowledge of the Lord Jesus. It is also true that our entire life is different! If we are what we've always been, we are not saved. I know that I am saved because on the seventh of May, 1974, I received the Lord Jesus Christ as my Savior and also because I have never gotten over it! And it is not that we are trying to be saved. If I asked you, "Are you an elephant?" You would not say, "Well, I'm trying to be!" You either are an elephant or you're not. No one who is trying to be saved understands salvation. *You are either saved or you're not!* You are saved because you have had a personal, life-changing encounter with the Lord Jesus Christ at a point in time. It is a matter of trusting not trying.

So Are You Ready to Be Saved?

If this is something you want to do, then here is a suggested prayer; the words are not what's important but what's in your heart. If God is dealing with you, then cry out to Him:

Lord Jesus, I need you. Thank you for dying on the cross for my sins. I cannot save myself. I cannot even help you save me. But the best I know how, I confess that I am a sinner and believe that the Lord Jesus Christ died on the cross for my sins and rose from the dead. I open the door of my life and receive you right now as my Savior. Come in and make me the kind of person you want me to be.

If you just received the Lord Jesus Christ as your Savior, then you are saved! This promise is based on the authority of God's Word.

"But as many as received Him, to them He gave the right to become children of

God, to those who believe in His name" (John 1:12).

Made in the
USA
Columbia, SC